3.4

Animals and Their Eggs

For a free color catalog describing Gareth Stevens' list of high-quality books and multimedia programs, call 1-800-542-2595 (USA) or 1-800-461-9120 (Canada). Gareth Stevens Publishing's Fax: (414) 332-3567.

Library of Congress Cataloging-in-Publication Data available upon request from publisher. Fax: (414) 332-3567 for the attention of the Publishing Records Department.

ISBN 0-8368-2714-7

This North American edition first published in 2000 by
Gareth Stevens Publishing
A World Almanac Education Group Company
330 West Olive Street, Suite 100
Milwaukee, WI 53212 USA

This U.S. edition © 2000 by Gareth Stevens, Inc.
First published as *Ik Kom Uit Een Ei* with an original
© 1996 by Mozaïek, an imprint of Uitgeverij Clavis, Hasselt.
Additional end matter © 2000 by Gareth Stevens, Inc.

Text and illustrations: Renne
English translation: Alison Taurel
English text: Dorothy L. Gibbs
Gareth Stevens series editor: Dorothy L. Gibbs
Editorial assistant: Diane Laska-Swanke

Printed in the United States of America

1 2 3 4 5 6 7 8 9 04 03 02 01 00

Animals and Their Eggs

Renne

Gareth Stevens Publishing
A WORLD ALMANAC EDUCATION GROUP COMPANY

This baby bird came out of an egg.

What exactly is an egg?

An egg is like a small house in which a living creature, such as a bird, develops.

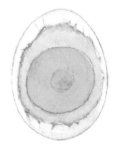 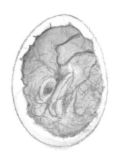 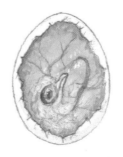 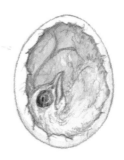 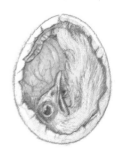

An egg provides food, shelter, and protection. Eggs have many enemies. Lots of animals like to eat them, and eggs are not always safe against rain, snow, heat, and mold.

All birds come from eggs.

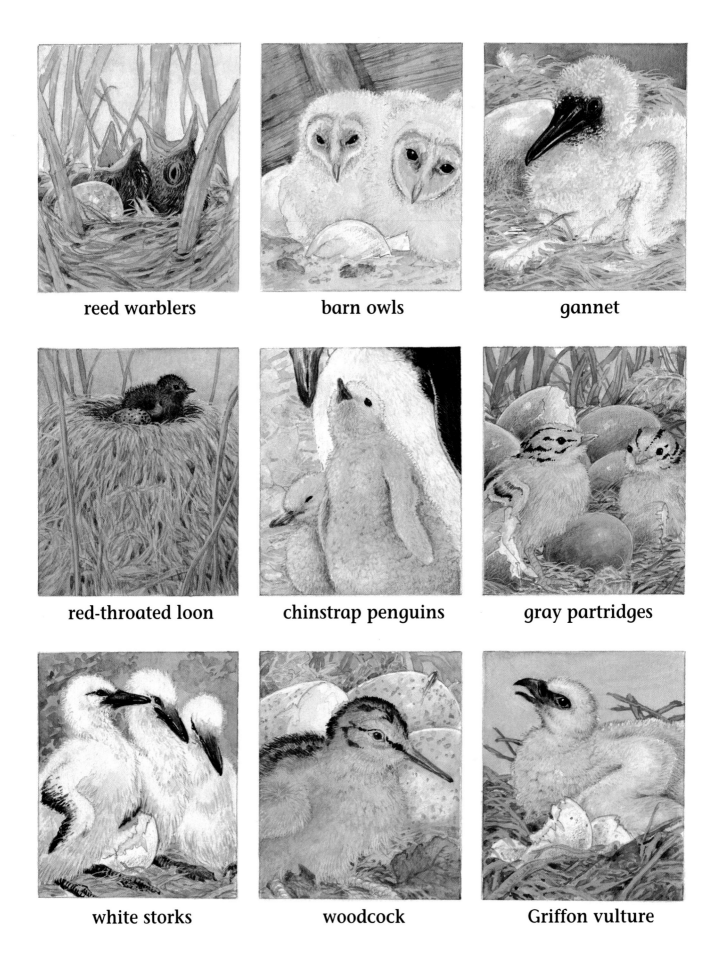

reed warblers

barn owls

gannet

red-throated loon

chinstrap penguins

gray partridges

white storks

woodcock

Griffon vulture

house martins

ducks

ostrich

wood pigeon

kingfishers

cuckoo

golden eagle

bee hummingbird

emus

The eggs of one kind of bird usually look different from the eggs of another kind of bird. Some, however, look exactly alike.

These eggs are from:

1. a hummingbird
2. a parakeet
3. a thrush
4. a white stork
5. a mute swan
6. an ostrich

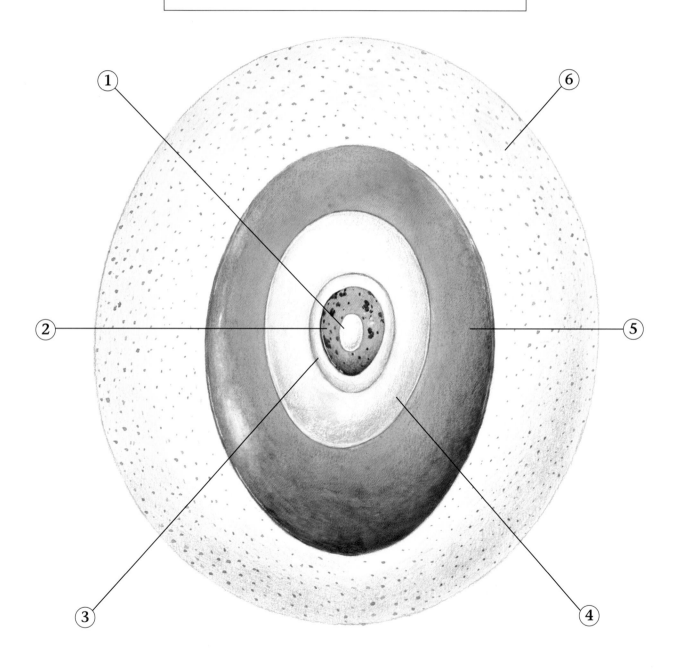

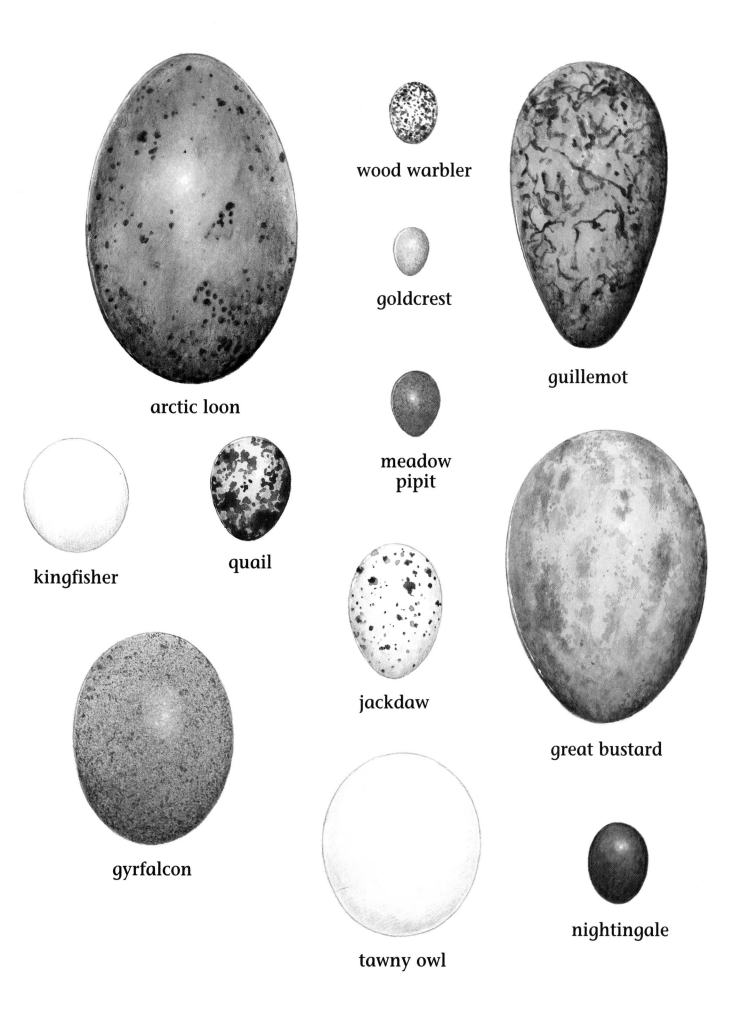

wood warbler

goldcrest

guillemot

arctic loon

meadow
pipit

kingfisher

quail

jackdaw

great bustard

gyrfalcon

nightingale

tawny owl

A hummingbird egg is
the smallest in the world.

An ostrich egg is the largest.

Just as the eggs of birds might look
different, their babies, or chicks, also
might look different. Some chicks
leave their nests shortly after they
hatch and search for food themselves.
Other chicks stay in the nest and
are cared for by their parents.

goldeneye duck

northern shoveler ducks

water rail

ring-necked pheasants

plover

mute swan

skylarks

purple
swamphen

ruff

Birds are not the only creatures that come from eggs.

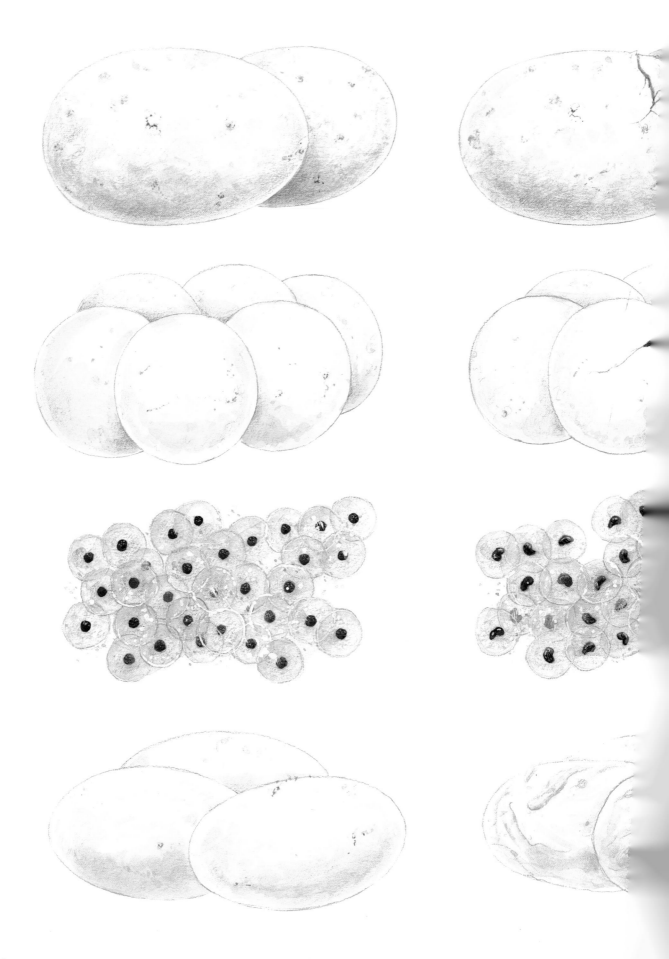

Reptiles and amphibians also come from eggs.
Their eggs have soft, parchmentlike shells.

When baby sea turtles come
out of their eggs, they crawl
to the sea all by themselves.
Unfortunately, they are
often caught by predators.

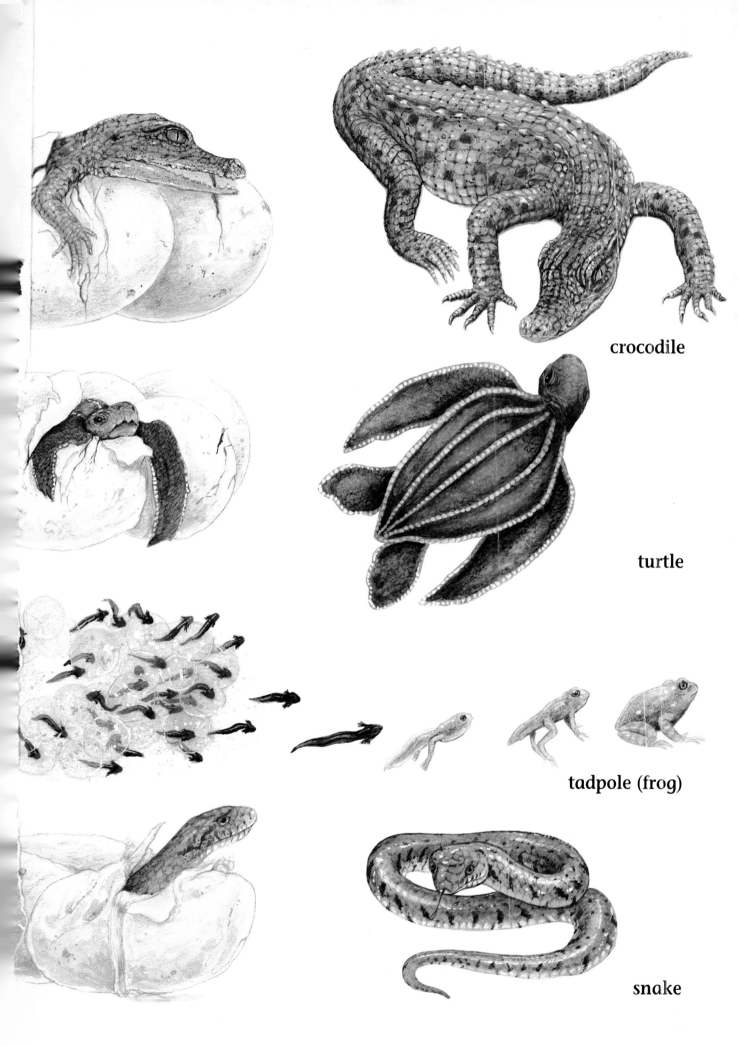

crocodile

turtle

tadpole (frog)

snake

What kinds of animals are coming out of these eggs?

A mother crocodile keeps
a close watch over her
eggs and her young.

One kind of snake digs a ho[le]
in which to lay its eggs an[d]
hatches the eggs itse[lf]

Many animals in the sea come from eggs —
fish, starfish, worms, shellfish.

These are the eggs of the

dogfish shark

octopus

squid

shrimp

Whales are mammals. Instead of laying eggs like most other sea animals, they give birth to their young.

A butterfly comes from
an egg — well, almost!

The larva, or caterpillar, of a
butterfly comes out of an egg . . .

and turns into a butterfly.

Butterfly eggs look like beautiful stones. They come in many shapes, colors, and textures, and they are often found stuck to the leaves of plants.

Most insects lay eggs.
Only a few insects give birth to their young.

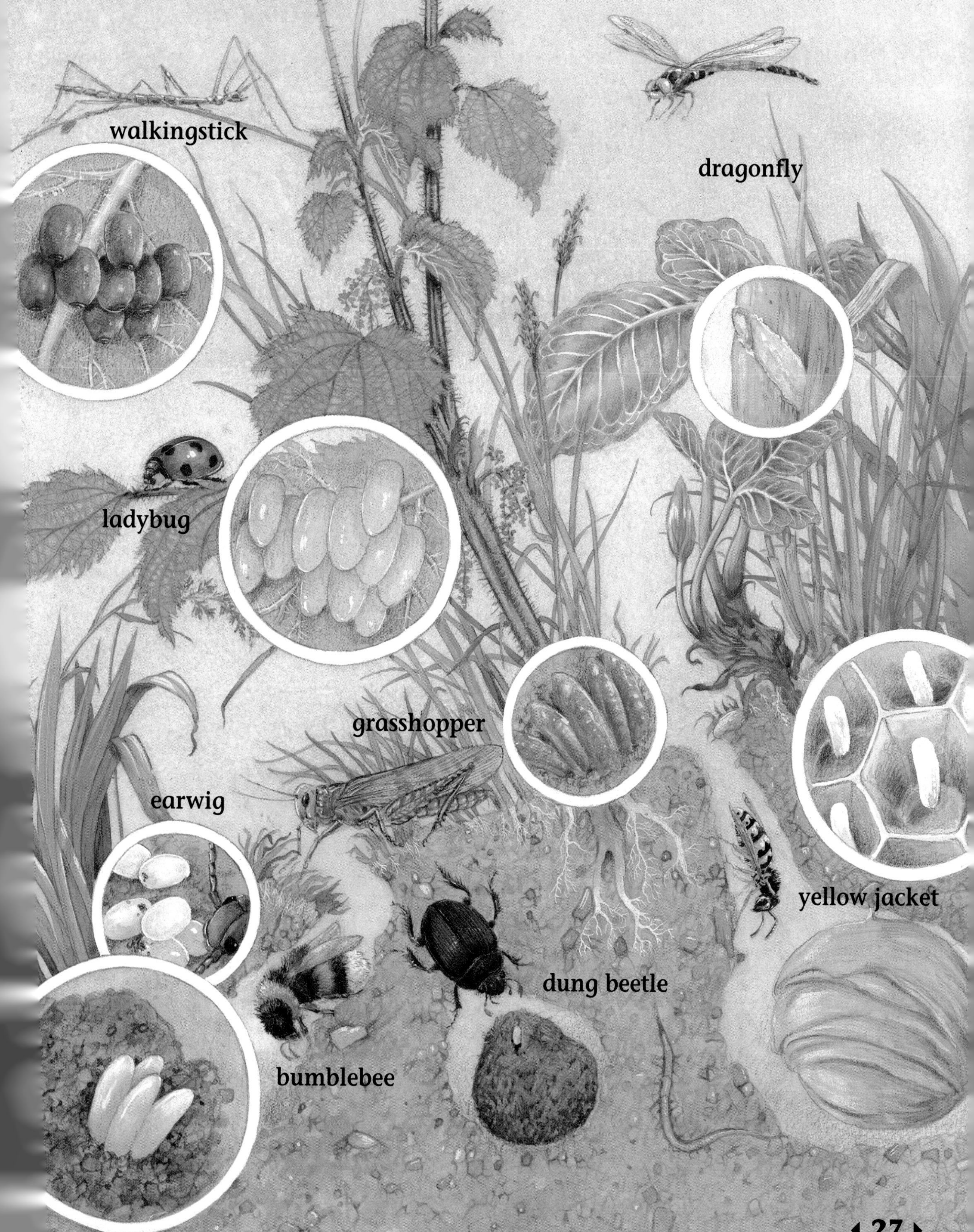

walkingstick

dragonfly

ladybug

grasshopper

earwig

yellow jacket

bumblebee

dung beetle

After insects lay their eggs, they usually leave the young to fend for themselves. Social insects, such as ants and bees, are the best at taking care of their eggs.

ants

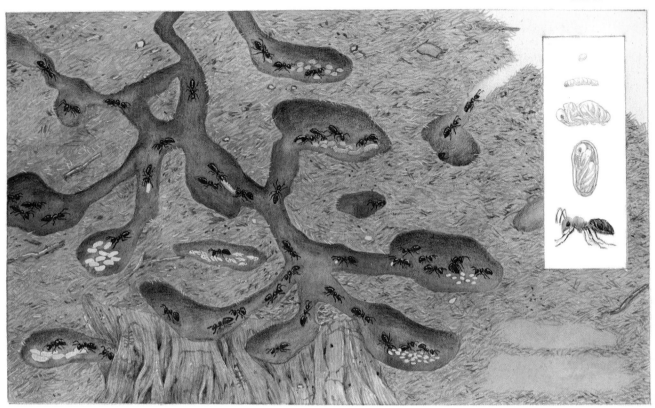

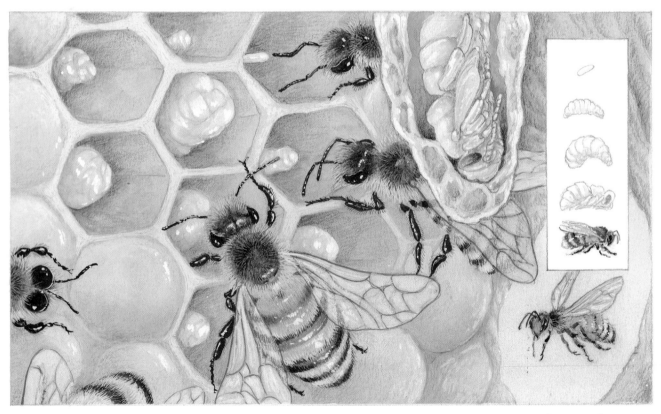

honeybees

When wasp eggs hatch, the queen that laid them takes care of the larvae herself. Termite eggs are laid by a queen, but workers take care of them and tend the larvae.

potter wasp

termites

Although these insects are not social insects,
they, too, take good care of their eggs.

An earwig even licks
its eggs clean.

Spiders are not insects,
but they keep a close
watch over their eggs.

The dung beetle makes a
dung ball for its larvae.

spider eggs

Shield bugs cover their eggs
with their bodies to protect them.

All of these insects lay eggs.

green lacewing

common blue butterfly

wood wasp

hawkmoth

blowfly

ladybug

six-spot burnet moth

grasshopper

bumble bee

mayfly

red admiral butterfly

spittlebug

dragonfly

peacock butterfly

rose chafer

firebug

ladybug larva

rhinoceros beetle

paper wasp

red wood ant

spotted fritillary butterfly larva

A duck-billed platypus lays eggs,
too — but it is a mammal!

Besides the platypus, the
hedgehog is the only other
mammal that lays eggs.

a platypus egg

a baby platypus

Although no other mammals lay eggs,
all mammals still produce eggs.

The eggs of a mammal stay inside the mother's body, where baby mammals develop until they are born. With few exceptions, then, we could say that **all** living creatures come from eggs.

Glossary

amphibian: an animal that is able to live either on land or in the water. A frog is an amphibian. Adult amphibians normally breathe air with lungs, but young amphibians, or larvae, usually have gills and can breathe only in water.

birth: (n) the appearance of new life that has come directly out of the body of its parent; give birth to: (v) to produce young that are alive when they come out of the parent's body, in contrast to young that develop in and hatch from an egg.

dung: the waste that comes out of an animal's body; an animal's droppings.

fend: to protect and provide for oneself; to get along without any help from others.

hatch: to come into the world, or be born, by coming out of an egg. The young of birds, fish, and many insects hatch from eggs.

larva: the wormlike form of most young insects, and some other animals without a backbone, at the time they hatch. A caterpillar is the larva of a butterfly or a moth. A tadpole is the larva of a frog. A larva often goes through several stages of development before it reaches its adult form.

mammal: an animal with a backbone and hair or fur on its body. A female mammal usually gives birth to live young and feeds them with milk from her body.

mold: a growth of fungus that forms a fuzzy coating often found on spoiled food as well as on some damp surfaces.

parchmentlike: resembling the translucent, or somewhat see-through, writing paper made from the skins of animals such as sheep and goats.

predator: an animal that hunts and eats other animals. An owl is a predator that hunts and eats mice.

protection: the act of being covered or shielded from danger or harm.

reptile: an air-breathing animal that has a backbone and, usually, slimy or scaly skin. A reptile moves by sliding on its belly, like a snake, or crawling along on very short legs, like a lizard. Crocodiles and turtles are reptiles — even most dinosaurs were reptiles.

shellfish: an animal that has a shell and lives in water. Many shellfish are very good to eat. Lobsters, crabs, and clams are shellfish.

shelter: a covered or shielded place that provides protection from dangers or discomforts, such as bad weather.

social: living together or having cooperative relationships with others, as members of a species, group, or colony.

texture: the look and feel of any kind of surface, such as the ridges on split wood, the weave of fabric, or the grit of sandpaper.

More Books to Read

Birds, Nests, and Eggs. Caterpillars, Bugs, and Butterflies. Young Naturalist Field Guides (series). Mel Boring (Gareth Stevens)

DK Nature Encyclopedia. (Dorling Kindersley)

Egg. Robert Burton (Dorling Kindersley)

Fish. Our Living World (series). Edward R. Ricciuti (Blackbirch)

From Egg to Chicken. Lifecycles (series). Gerald Legg (Franklin Watts)

How Animals Protect Themselves. Animal Survival (series). Michel Barré (Gareth Stevens)

Insect Metamorphosis: From Egg to Adult. Ron and Nancy Goor (Atheneum)

A New Frog: My First Look at the Life Cycle of an Amphibian. Pamela Hickman and Heather Collins (Kids Can Press)

The Science of Birds. The Science of Insects. The Science of Reptiles. Living Science (series). Janice Parker (Gareth Stevens)

Videos

All About Animal Life Cycles. (Schlessinger Media)

Animal Eggs. Henry's Amazing Animals (series). (Library Video)

Animal Families: Mother Nature. (Questar, Inc.)

The Demands of the Egg. The Life of Birds (Vol. 4). (Twentieth Century Fox Home Entertainment)

Sea Turtle Adventures. Audubon's Animal Adventure (series). (Library Video)

Web Sites

Eggs — A Virtual Exhibition. *www.pma.edmonton.ab.ca/vexhibit/eggs/vexhome/egghome.htm*

Entomology for Beginners. *www1.bos.nl/homes/bijlmakers/entomology/begin.htm*

Platypus. *home.mira.net/~areadman/plat.htm*

Tortoise Trust: Eggs F.A.Q. *www.tortoisetrust.org/articles/eggfaq.html*

To find additional Web sites, use a reliable search engine with one or more of the following keywords: *fish, freshwater animals, invertebrates, marine animals, marine life, penguins, reptiles, seabirds, swimming insects,* and *whales.*

Index